STETSON

NEW HAVEN FREE PUBLIC LIBRARY

3 5000 06885 1749

MAR 9 2001

OFFICIALLY WITHDRAWN
NEW HAVEN FREE PUBLIC LIBRARY

D1530472

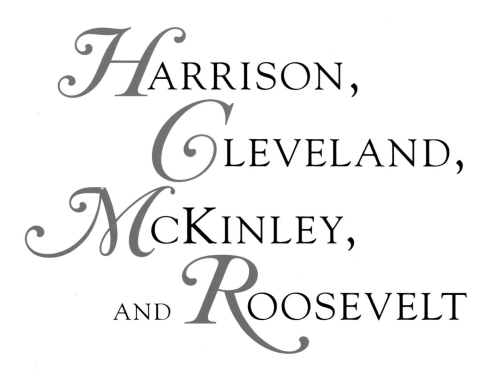

Harrison, Cleveland, McKinley, and Roosevelt

by

RICHARD STEINS

VOLUME

7

ROURKE CORPORATION, INC.
VERO BEACH, FLORIDA 32964

© 1997 by Rourke Corporation, Inc.

All rights reserved. No part of this book may be reproduced or utilized in any form or by any means, electronic or mechanical including photocopying, recording, or by any information storage and retrieval system without permission in writing from the publisher.

Printed in the United States of America.

A Blackbirch Graphics book.
Series Editor: Tanya Lee Stone
Editors: Elizabeth Taylor, Lisa Clyde Nielsen
Art Director: Sonja Kalter
Production Editor/Design: Laura S. Patchkofsky

Photo Credits
Cover: Benjamin Harrison and Grover Cleveland, White House Historical Association; William McKinley, National Portrait Gallery; Theodore Roosevelt, Library of Congress.
Pages 4, 12, 15, 21, 24, 30, 35, 38, 45, 49, 50: Brown Brothers; pages 6, 32, 46: AP/Wide World Photos, Inc.; pages 8, 9, 26: National Portrait Gallery; pages 10, 18: White House Historical Association; pages 14, 20, 23, 31, 36, 41, 42: Library of Congress; pages 16, 44, 53: North Wind Picture Archives.

Library of Congress Cataloging-in-Publication Data

Weber, Michael, 1945-
    The complete history of our presidents / Michael Weber, Richard Steins, Eileen Lucas.
       p. cm.
    Includes bibliographical references and index.
    Summary: Discusses the political lives and times of the men who served as United States presidents, their administrations, and the events which occurred during their tenures.
    ISBN 0-86593-405-3 (set)
    1. Presidents—United States—Juvenile literature.
[1. Presidents.]   I. Steins, Richard.   II. Lucas, Eileen.
III. Title.
E176.1.W365   1997
973'.099—DC20

96-14831
CIP
AC
Rev.

WILLIS K. STETSON
BRANCH LIBRARY

j923.1
COMPLETE
v.7

TABLE OF CONTENTS

In the early 1900s, overcrowding in New York City—pictured here—and other U.S. cities created unpleasant living conditions.

1
★ ★ ★

America in the 1890s and Early 1900s

America in the 1890s was a rapidly growing nation that was fast becoming a major industrial power. As the factory system spread to more and more industries, cities began to swell. Immigrants from abroad swarmed into the cities looking for jobs. In addition, young men and women from America's farms turned to the cities as well. Agriculture had become mechanized—that is, it had become a big business—and small farmers could not compete with large, machine-operated farms. America's farmers found it increasingly difficult to make a living, and they tended to blame bankers and the wealthy classes for their problems. Conditions of overcrowding and other social ills came with the increase of population in the cities.

The 1890s were a time of protest and reform. From the farms to the cities, people demanded change. Still, the majority of reformers wanted to make the existing system better, not destroy it.

The Progressive Movement

The reform movement that tried to address America's problems was called Progressivism. It began in the 1890s in the cities, where the problems were most severe. Dedicated men and women from middle-class backgrounds voluntarily moved into the slums and established "settlement houses." These were places where poor people could go for help and to learn skills. Among the most famous leaders of the early settlement houses was Jane Addams, who founded Hull House in Chicago.

Other Progressives turned their attention to attacking corruption in local governments. They formed nonpartisan leagues, which meant that they did not belong to any one political party. These leagues wanted to defeat people and organizations that had held power for a long time. During the 1890s, many reform mayors

Jane Addams established one of the first settlement houses in America. Here, she meets with young people outside of Hull House.

were elected throughout the country. They were dedicated to improving city services and to cleaning up the slums.

These early reformers were often frustrated, however. For the most part, the state legislatures were controlled by the railroad owners and their interests, and attempts to block reforms in the cities were frequent. The Progressives then developed a new strategy and turned to state politics to take control of a number of important state governments. One of the most famous of these reformers was Robert La Follette, who served as governor of Wisconsin (1901–1906).

La Follette and other Progressive governors passed a number of important reforms: They established direct primaries, the secret ballot, and the direct election of senators. They also increased state regulation of the railroads and raised taxes on big corporations. To correct the worst features of industrialization, the Progressives passed workmen's compensation laws to protect the rights of workers, banned child labor, and established minimum wages in industry.

Progressives and the Presidency

In order to obtain its goals at the federal level, the Progressive movement needed to elect a president who sympathized with its principles. For much of the 1890s, the Progressives made little headway. Benjamin Harrison, a Republican president who served from 1889 to 1893, was a true conservative who had little understanding of, or sympathy for, the reform movement.

Grover Cleveland, a Democrat whose second term spanned the years 1893 to 1897, was a man who favored reform. But he was mainly conservative and did not believe that the government should play as active a role in social affairs as the Progressives thought it should. In many respects, Cleveland did not differ from his Republican predecessors in his beliefs about the role of the government.

★ ★

Jane Addams: Progressive Reformer

Jane Addams

Jane Addams was born in Cedarville, Illinois, in 1860. In 1889, she and a friend, Ellen Gates Starr, founded Hull House in Chicago, Illinois. It was one of the first settlement houses in the United States. Settlement houses served as community centers for the poor and later became centers for social reform. Hull House became important in civic affairs in Chicago and was a model for other settlement houses that opened throughout America in the 1890s.

Jane Addams was a true Progressive reformer. Although her primary objective was to help the poor improve their lives, she also developed interests in other kinds of reform. She became a leader in the woman suffrage movement and was also a pacifist (a person opposed to war). In 1931, Jane Addams was awarded the Nobel Peace Prize. She died in 1935 at the age of 75.

William McKinley, a Republican, was also conservative regarding domestic (American) affairs, and he did little to advance the Progressive domestic agenda. He was largely concerned with foreign affairs, and during his term of office—1897 to 1901—the United States acquired many overseas territories. The Progressives were in favor of America's playing an important role in the world. They believed that Americans should offer aid to poor foreigners just as they should help the less well-off in their own country. The Progressives did agree with some of McKinley's foreign-affair policies.

McKinley was assassinated in 1901 and was succeeded by the young and impulsive Theodore Roosevelt. When Roosevelt took on the big corporate trusts and became known as a trust-buster, the Progressives thought that they finally had one of their own in the highest office in the land.

Roosevelt, however, was willing to support only parts of the Progressive program, and throughout his presidency—1901 to 1909—Congress remained extremely conservative and resistant to Progressive reforms. Moreover, Roosevelt was not willing to fight Congress on each and every issue. And much of his time was spent on foreign affairs, particularly on expanding America's role overseas.

The Presidency in the Twentieth Century

The four presidents who lived in the White House between 1889 and 1909 took the nation into the twentieth century. Benjamin Harrison represented the kind of president the country had become accustomed to in the years after the Civil War. He believed that the best government was one that governed the least amount possible.

Twenty years later, however, the nation had grown used to a youthful and vigorous president who threw himself into the center of almost every conflict. Theodore Roosevelt was an activist president, one well-suited to facing the challenges of the twentieth century. He believed that the best government was one that played an active role at home and abroad. In that sense, he was truly a Progressive because he believed that action would change things for the better.

As president, Theodore Roosevelt helped to pass some reforms that were supported by Progressives.

Benjamin Harrison
23rd President of the United States

Term: *March 4, 1889–March 4, 1893; Republican*
First Lady: *Caroline Lavinia Scott Harrison*
Vice-President: *Levi P. Morton*

2

★ ★ ★

Benjamin Harrison

Benjamin Harrison came from a long line of American patriots. His great-grandfather, also named Benjamin Harrison, had signed the Declaration of Independence in 1776. His grandfather, William Henry Harrison, was the ninth president of the United States (he died in office in 1841, only 30 days after his inauguration). Benjamin Harrison was quiet and dignified, and he hated the rough-and-tumble of politics. Nevertheless, on the rainy morning of March 4, 1889, he found himself standing on the steps of the Capitol, taking the oath of office as the 23rd president of the United States.

Early Life

Benjamin Harrison was born in North Bend, Ohio, on August 20, 1833, the second son of John Scott Harrison and Elizabeth Irwin Harrison. In his mid-teens, Benjamin attended a small preparatory school near Cincinnati. In his junior year, he began attending Miami University in Oxford, Ohio. One reason for the move was the interest he had taken in the daughter of one of his professors, Dr. John Scott. Caroline Lavinia Scott (known as Carrie) was an outgoing and fun-loving person—very much the opposite of the serious Benjamin—and he was infatuated with her.

By the time Benjamin graduated from Miami University in 1852, he and Carrie had become engaged. They were married in 1853 and moved to Indianapolis, Indiana.

Lawyer and Soldier

Harrison had studied law in Cincinnati, and, after moving to Indianapolis, he opened his own law practice. But clients were difficult to find. Harrison had to take a low-paying job at the Indiana Supreme Court and move his family into an inexpensive boardinghouse. By 1858, the Harrisons had two young children—Russell and Mary.

Benjamin Harrison led a regiment of volunteers during the Civil War.

Benjamin Harrison joined the newly founded Republican party in 1856. He was opposed to slavery, and when the Civil War broke out in 1861, Harrison volunteered his services. The governor accepted his offer to recruit a regiment from Indiana, and gradually a group of volunteers was assembled in Indianapolis. Harrison studied military tactics and drilled his men. They came to regard him with great affection and nicknamed him Little Ben.

★ ★

The 70th Regiment of Indiana Volunteers took part in Union general William Tecumseh Sherman's attack on Atlanta, Georgia, and saw action in a number of other battles. By the time the war ended in 1865, Harrison had earned the rank of brigadier general.

Political Career

In the years immediately following the war, Harrison returned to his job at the Indiana Supreme Court and to his law practice. In the North, Civil War veterans were very popular with the public. Harrison—like many other veterans—was regarded as an attractive candidate for public office. In 1876, he was nominated by the Republicans to run for governor of Indiana. But Harrison was a poor campaigner; he found it difficult to appear relaxed in public. Because he feared catching a cold, he wore gloves wherever he went. His opponents made fun of him, taunting him with the name Kid-Glove Harrison. In his first try for high office, Harrison was defeated.

Four years later, however, the Indiana legislature did elect Harrison to the U.S. Senate. As a former army man, he supported many of the numerous pension bills for army veterans that came before the Senate during the 1880s. In 1886, he was not re-elected. His political career seemed to be over.

The Election of 1888

When the Republicans gathered in 1888 to choose their candidate for president, the field seemed to be wide open. Senator James G. Blaine—the unsuccessful opponent in 1884 of Democrat Grover Cleveland—was unwilling to run again. In this atmosphere of uncertainty, Harrison seemed like a candidate around whom all Republicans could rally. He was a Civil War veteran, a former senator, and the grandson of a former president. The

★ ★

First Lady Caroline Harrison

Caroline Lavinia Scott was born in Oxford, Ohio, in 1832. She was the second daughter of the Reverend John Scott and his wife, Mary Neal. Her father was a Presbyterian minister and educator who founded the Oxford Female Institute, a school for girls. He was also a professor at Miami University in Ohio. It was there that Caroline met her future husband—one of her father's students, the young Benjamin Harrison.

In the early years of their marriage, Caroline and Benjamin lived in Indianapolis, where he struggled to establish his law practice. She helped raise their children and did volunteer work at the local Presbyterian church and at an orphanage.

In the spring of 1889, the Harrisons moved into the White House. They were accompanied by several family members, including their daughter Mary and her two children; Mrs. Harrison's aged father; and her niece Mary Dimmick. Periodically, their son Russell and his children would come to live in the White House as well.

Mrs. Harrison was concerned about the condition of the White House, which she felt needed to be renovated. She succeeded in persuading Congress to fund the project. As part of the renovation, electricity was installed in the mansion. (The Harrisons, however, were afraid of getting electrical shocks. So they hired an electrician whose job it was to turn lights off and on for them.)

The First Lady began the White House china collection, to which every presidential family since has added. In addition, she was one of the founders of the Daughters of the American Revolution, a patriotic women's organization dedicated to performing charitable work. She also agreed to help raise money for The Johns Hopkins University Medical School, on the condition that it admit women.

Mrs. Harrison's health began to decline late in 1891. She developed tuberculosis. At that time, this disease was incurable. On October 25, 1892, only 11 days before the presidential election, she died in the White House. A funeral service was held in the East Room, and her body was returned to Indianapolis for burial. During her final illness, she had been helped by her niece Mary Dimmick, who would later become Benjamin Harrison's second wife.

Caroline Lavinia Scott Harrison

convention nominated him for president and chose a New York banker, Levi P. Morton, to run for vice-president.

On Election Day, President Cleveland actually got over 100,000 votes more than did Harrison. Harrison's votes, however, were concentrated in states with more electoral votes. Because the president is elected by the Electoral College and not by the popular vote, Harrison won, with 233 electoral votes to Cleveland's 168.

Levi P. Morton became the Republican candidate for vice-president in 1888.

President Harrison

Harrison was a serious and dignified president, but he never achieved great popularity—either with the people or within the Republican party. Still, Harrison approved all of the major Republican measures that came out of Congress. The McKinley Tariff Act of 1890, which Harrison signed, was favored by most big businesses because it put in place high tariffs that protected American industry from foreign competition.

In 1890, the president approved the Sherman Silver Purchase Act. This measure was designed to keep the price of silver high by having the government buy all the silver available in the

During Harrison's term, the government's purchase of silver and the hoarding of gold by citizens set the stage for economic crisis in the 1890s. Here, a political cartoon presents a humorous look at the crisis.

United States. Despite this act, the price of silver did not rise, because worldwide production remained high. Cheap silver began to pile up in the U.S. Treasury, while the amount of gold in circulation decreased. This economic decline cast a shadow over Harrison's last year in office.

During Harrison's presidency, six new states were admitted to the Union: North Dakota, South Dakota, Montana, Washington,

★ ★

Wyoming, and Idaho. In addition, the Oklahoma Territory was opened for white settlement in 1889 (prior to that, it had been reserved for Indians).

Despite all these important gains, as the election of 1892 approached, the Democrats sensed that they might have an opportunity to recapture the White House from the unpopular Harrison. They renominated former president Cleveland, while the Republicans renominated Harrison. The election was not even close. Cleveland won 277 Electoral College votes to Harrison's 145.

In the final days of the campaign, tragedy struck the Harrison family. On October 25, 1892, only 11 days before the election, First Lady Caroline Harrison died in the White House after a long illness.

After the White House

The widowed and defeated president returned to his home in Indiana in March 1893. He returned to his law practice and wrote for national magazines. He also began work on a book about the federal government. That work, entitled *This Country of Ours*, was published in 1897. (His *Views of an Ex-President* was published after he died.)

In 1896, Harrison married Mary Dimmick, a niece of his late wife's who had helped nurse the ailing First Lady during her final days. In 1897, when the ex-president was 64 years old, he and his new wife became parents. Mrs. Harrison gave birth to a daughter, whom they named Elizabeth. Harrison lived another four years before dying at the age of 67 on March 13, 1901. He was buried in Indianapolis beside his first wife.

★ ★

Grover Cleveland
24th President of the United States

Term: *March 4, 1893–March 4, 1897; Democratic*
First Lady: *Frances Folsom Cleveland*
Vice-President: *Adlai E. Stevenson*

3

★ ★ ★

Grover Cleveland

Grover Cleveland was the 22nd president (*see Volume 6*) *and* the 24th president. After his first term, which ended on March 4, 1889, he settled in New York, where he resumed the practice of law. But Cleveland was not done with politics. As he and his wife Frances had left the White House in 1889, Mrs. Cleveland had predicted, "We'll be back."

In 1892, the Democrats took the first step toward making that prediction a reality. Realizing that the incumbent Republican president was unpopular and vulnerable, they renominated Cleveland for a third time. Cleveland was still popular with the people. In fact, he had not lost the popular vote in 1888. Cleveland had lost the election in the Electoral College, where Harrison

Adlai E. Stevenson became Cleveland's vice-president during his second term.

had won more votes. The Democrats chose Adlai E. Stevenson of Illinois, a former assistant postmaster general during Cleveland's first term, to be his vice-presidential running mate.

Unlike the election four years earlier, the 1892 contest was not even close. Cleveland received almost 400,000 votes more than Harrison did and prevailed in the Electoral College by a vote of 277 to 145. However, the 1892 election was complicated by the presence of a third party: the People's party, known as the Populists. The Populists spoke for the discontented farmers of the Midwest and the West. They nominated James Weaver as their presidential candidate and won more than 1 million popular votes and 22 electoral votes. They failed in their objective to win more votes than the Democrats. Nonetheless, within four years, many Populist programs were adopted by the Democrats.

Economic Crisis

The goodwill and optimism that accompanied Cleveland's return to the White House lasted only a few months. In the spring of 1893, the country was plunged into a financial crisis that led to an economic depression.

★ ★

First Lady Frances Cleveland

Frances Folsom was born in Buffalo, New York, in 1864, the only child of Oscar Folsom and Emma C. Harmon Folsom. Her father was a law partner of Grover Cleveland's. When Oscar Folsom died, Grover Cleveland became the court-appointed administrator of the Folsom estate. In this position, Cleveland guided young Frances's education.

When Frances entered Wells College in 1882, Cleveland asked Mrs. Folsom's permission to correspond with her. During her years in college, they exchanged letters, and Cleveland frequently sent her flowers. Despite a 27-year difference in their ages, the relationship blossomed into a romance. Cleveland proposed, and the couple was married in the White House in June 1886.

At 21, Frances Cleveland became the youngest First Lady—and something of a novelty. Invitations to the White House became highly valued. Mrs. Cleveland began the practice of having two receptions a week, one of which was held on Saturday afternoons so that working women could attend. Her youth and charm won her immediate popularity throughout the country.

Even though Cleveland was defeated for re-election in 1888, Frances believed that they would eventually return to the White House for a second term. They moved to New York in the spring of 1889, and two years later, their first child, Ruth, was born.

In 1892, Mrs. Cleveland's prediction came true. Cleveland was re-elected, and the family moved back into the White House on March 4, 1893. Their daughters Esther and Marion were born in the White House during Cleveland's second term.

It was also during this term that the Clevelands decided that the White House was too public a place to raise children. Desiring privacy, they bought a new house, along the Potomac River, two miles from Washington, D.C. The family lived there from April until December each year. During the winter months—the social season in Washington—they lived in the White House.

Two sons were born after Cleveland left the presidency on March 4, 1897. The family moved to Princeton, New Jersey, where the former president died in 1908.

Frances Cleveland remarried in 1913. Her second husband, Thomas J. Preston, Jr., was a professor of archaeology at Princeton. The former First Lady lived an active life until her death at the age of 83 in 1947.

Frances Folsom Cleveland

The event that triggered the collapse was called the Panic of 1893. Under President Harrison, the government had been buying silver. At the same time, people began hoarding gold. As more and more gold was pulled out of circulation, the Treasury lost its gold reserves, threatening its backing of the money in circulation. Consequently, people lost confidence in the economy, causing banks to fail, and railroads began to go bankrupt. Farmers lost their farms because they could not meet the payments on their mortgages.

Cleveland called a special session of Congress to deal with the economic crisis. A large number of Democrats wanted him to end the gold standard (gold backing all paper money and coins) and authorize the unlimited production of silver coins. Cleveland, however, was a firm believer in the gold standard and supported the repeal of the Sherman Silver Purchase Act.

There was practically no gold in the Treasury, and in order to get money to buy some, Cleveland turned to wealthy Wall Street bankers for a loan. The bankers agreed to lend the government money so that gold could be purchased for the Treasury. Many people were shocked that the government of the United States had to be bailed out of its financial problems by wealthy Wall Street businessmen.

Labor Unrest

As the economic depression worsened, the country was wracked by strikes and other labor unrest. Strikers demanding higher wages and better working conditions walked off their jobs in the textile mills and the coal mines. But the most troubling actions, from Cleveland's point of view, were the railroad strikes. The railroads were vital to the continued operation of the American economy. Any shutdown was a threat to the well-being of the country as a whole.

★ ★

In 1894, the American Railway Union (ARU) came to the aid of railroad workers who were striking against the Pullman Palace Car Company, which manufactured railroad cars. The Pullman workers were striking to protest a wage cut and the firing of colleagues who were union members. The ARU, headed by Eugene V. Debs, a Socialist, called for a boycott of Pullman cars. Soon, 50,000 railroad workers were honoring the Pullman workers' strike and refusing to run the railroads. Within days, all rail traffic into and out of Chicago, a major rail hub, had come to a halt.

The railroad owners appealed to the government to step in and end the strike. On July 4, 1894, Cleveland sent in federal troops. Much bloodshed and rioting fol-

In 1894, Eugene V. Debs led a strike of railroad workers that halted train traffic in Chicago.

lowed, but the troops quickly crushed the strike. Debs and other union leaders were arrested for violating a federal court order to end the strike. The Pullman strike was one of the low points of Cleveland's second term. The popularity the president had enjoyed shortly after his re-election declined as people began to view him as a strikebreaker.

President Cleveland and his Cabinet in 1893

Foreign Affairs

When Cleveland returned to the White House in 1893, he was an experienced president used to making his own decisions. Thus, in foreign affairs, as in other matters, Cleveland made policy decisions without turning to his advisors for assistance. His Cabinet contained no powerful or dominant figures. For example, his secretary of state was Walter Q. Gersham, a competent but undynamic public official who had served President Chester A. Arthur as postmaster general and secretary of the treasury.

Cleveland remained a strong opponent of U.S. expansion. In 1893, he withdrew a treaty from the Senate that would have authorized the annexation of Hawaii to the United States. In 1895, he discouraged American support for Cubans who were revolting against Spain, which owned and governed the island. Cleveland, however, was a strong supporter of the principles of the Monroe Doctrine. (The Monroe Doctrine was a policy stated by President James Monroe in 1823. It warned European nations not to attempt to colonize or interfere in the Western Hemisphere.) When Great Britain quarreled with Venezuela over its boundary with a neigboring British colony, Cleveland forcefully intervened and demanded that the British settle the dispute peacefully.

After the White House

Cleveland's policies were not supported by a large segment of the Democratic party. When it met to nominate a presidential candidate in 1896, the convention chose 36-year-old William Jennings Bryan of Nebraska, a strong supporter of the unlimited coinage of silver (so-called free silver) and a spokesperson for farmers of the Midwest. The convention also rejected support for the gold standard, a direct slap in the face for Cleveland.

The Republican candidate for president, William McKinley, defeated Bryan overwhelmingly in the election of 1896. Cleveland, an outcast in his party, retired from the White House for the second and last time on March 4, 1897. He and his wife bought a large home in Princeton, New Jersey, where he lived in retirement until his death on June 24, 1908, at the age of 71. Cleveland is buried in Princeton Cemetery beneath a modest monument that does not identify him as an American president.

★ ★

William McKinley
25th President of the United States

Term: *March 4, 1897–September 14, 1901; Republican*
First Lady: *Ida Saxton McKinley*
Vice-Presidents: *Garret A. Hobart and Theodore Roosevelt*

4
★ ★ ★

William McKinley

William McKinley served as president of the United States at a time when the country acquired many overseas territories after its victory in the Spanish-American War. Under McKinley, the United States became a genuine world power. McKinley was fortunate to be president at this time. Prosperity had returned to the United States following the economic depression earlier in the 1890s. As a result, McKinley enjoyed increasing popularity and was easily re-elected in 1900. However, he never enjoyed a full second term. He was shot and killed only six months after his second inauguration, the third American president in 36 years to be assassinated.

27

Early Life

William McKinley was born in Niles, Ohio, on January 29, 1843, the seventh child of William and Nancy McKinley. His father managed a blast furnace for smelting iron ore, and his mother was a homemaker active in the local Methodist church. As a young man, William (who was called Will by his family and friends) showed a gift for making speeches. At age 17, he attended college briefly in Pennsylvania but was forced to return home because of ill health. For the next two years, he taught in a country school and worked part-time at the post office.

When the Civil War broke out in 1861, Will enlisted in the 23rd Ohio Volunteers. The 19-year-old soldier served under Rutherford B. Hayes—a future president of the United States— at the Battle of Antietam in 1862. He was in charge of food supplies during the battle, and Hayes later praised him for his courage in doing his job under fire. By the end of the war, McKinley had been promoted to the rank of major.

Early Political Career

Following his discharge from the army, McKinley returned to Ohio to study law. He opened his first office in Canton, Ohio, in 1867 and soon became involved in local Republican politics. In 1869, he was elected prosecuting attorney and quickly acquired a reputation as a fiercely honest and courageous young politician. He often spoke out for unpopular causes; he defended, for example, the right of African Americans to vote.

While in Canton, McKinley met Ida Saxton, the daughter of a wealthy banker who was working as a teller in her father's bank. They fell in love and were married in 1871. By 1873, they had two daughters, Katherine and Ida.

The young attorney was considered a valuable political property by local Republicans, who predicted great things for him.

★ ★

In 1876, McKinley was elected to the U.S. House of Representatives, where he began a distinguished career that spanned the next 14 years. In Congress, he became the chief spokesperson for a high protective tariff (a tax on imports to help domestic manufacturing). This position endeared him to industrialists back home in Ohio, who wanted high tariffs as a means of protecting their industries from foreign competition. McKinley, however, genuinely believed that high tariffs were good for the nation as a whole.

McKinley eventually became chair of the powerful House Ways and Means Committee, where he helped write and pass the comprehensive McKinley Tariff Act of 1890. This law extended high tariffs to practically all major products manufactured in the United States. It turned out, however, to be an extremely unpopular measure with the voters because it raised prices, and in the election of 1890, the Republicans were beaten and McKinley was defeated.

Governor of Ohio

Despite his losing the election, McKinley was still considered a strong candidate for high public office. In Ohio, he had attracted the attention of a powerful industrialist-politician named Marcus A. Hanna, who put the might of the Ohio Republican party at McKinley's disposal. Hanna persuaded McKinley to run for governor of Ohio. McKinley won the 1891 election and was re-elected in 1893.

Hanna's real goal for McKinley, however, was the White House. While he was governor, McKinley toured the nation, speaking on behalf of Republican candidates and attacking the Democrats for having caused the Panic of 1893 and the economic depression that followed. McKinley's travels made him well known throughout the country. Back in Ohio, Hanna was skillfully managing a campaign that guaranteed McKinley's nomination for president

★ ★

Vice-President Garret A. Hobart

at the 1896 Republican Convention. By the time the convention gathered, McKinley's nomination was secured. Garret A. Hobart of New Jersey, a prominent lawyer and businessman, was nominated by the Republicans for vice-president.

The 1896 Campaign

The 1896 presidential campaign began with the Democrats bitterly divided. They turned to Williams Jennings Bryan of Nebraska, a powerful speaker who argued passionately for the cause of free silver. The people who supported it were generally poor and in debt. To them, free silver represented easy access to money. Bryan's backing was strongest among farmers and silver miners in the West and the South. McKinley continued to advocate the gold standard. Although he was backed by wealthy industrialists and bankers, middle-class people who feared economic instability also voted for him. Support for McKinley was strongest in the Midwest and the East and in the far West.

Bryan was one of the first modern campaigners. Unlike previous candidates, who felt that campaigning for the presidency was in poor taste, Bryan toured the nation, giving the same speech over and over.

Despite Bryan's extensive travels and impassioned speeches, the nation was not ready to turn to him. McKinley won almost 600,000 more popular votes than Bryan did and was elected with 271 Electoral College votes to Bryan's 176.

First Lady Ida McKinley

Ida Saxton was born in Canton, Ohio, in 1847, the elder daughter of a wealthy banker. She and her sister attended a finishing school in Pennsylvania. When they graduated, they were sent off on a grand tour of Europe as a present from their father.

Ida could have spent her time attending parties and social events, but she wanted more responsibility. Her father suggested that she take a job as a teller in his bank. While at a picnic in 1867, she met young William McKinley. He had just finished his service in the Civil War and moved to Canton to set up his law practice. After a two-year courtship, which began in 1869, Ida and William were married in January 1871.

In December of that year their first child, Katherine (Katie), was born. A second child, Ida, was born in 1873 but died at the age of four months. The strain of childbirth and the death of her second child seriously affected Ida's health. Then, when Katie died at the age of five in 1876, Mrs. McKinley collapsed both physically and emotionally. At this time, she was diagnosed with epilepsy. Thereafter, she frequently suffered from seizures. For the remainder of her life, Ida McKinley was ill.

After the McKinleys arrived at the White House in 1897, Mrs. McKinley attempted to perform some of the social duties of First Lady. She greeted guests while seated in a blue velvet chair rather than stand in a receiving line. She carried a bouquet of flowers, a way of indicating that she would not shake hands. At state dinners, Mrs. McKinley was always seated next to the president, who kept a watchful eye out for any possible seizures. Occasionally, she would have a seizure in public, at which point the president would cover her head with a large napkin until the seizure had passed. Although this seemed quite strange to many people, the McKinleys' guests and the public respected the First Lady's privacy and spoke only of her "fainting spells."

The assassination of President McKinley in 1901 was a terrible blow for his already frail wife. She returned to Canton and spent her remaining years living with her younger sister and paying daily visits to McKinley's grave. When she died at the age of 59 in 1907, she was buried beside her husband, in the McKinley Memorial Mausoleum in Canton.

Ida Saxton McKinley

President McKinley and the Spanish-American War

McKinley's first term was centered on foreign relations. The island of Cuba, 90 miles south of Florida, was a Spanish colony in the 1890s. Cuban rebels wanted freedom from Spain, but the Spanish were reluctant to give up their empire in the Caribbean. President Grover Cleveland had refused to support the rebels, but McKinley was more willing to get involved.

Hoping to protect Americans in Cuba in the event that war broke out between Spain and the Cuban rebels, McKinley sent the U.S. battleship *Maine* to Havana harbor. On the night of February 15, 1898, the *Maine* exploded and sank to the bottom of the harbor. Two hundred sixty American lives were lost. The American press immediately accused the Spanish of having blown up the ship. However, a U.S. naval inquiry and a separate Spanish investigation were never able to determine the cause of the blast.

The destruction of the Maine *caused a brief war between the United States and Spain.*

In April 1898, even though Spain had signaled to McKinley a willingness to negotiate, Congress authorized a blockade of Spanish ports. When Spain heard about the blockade, it declared war on the United States.

The Spanish-American War was brief and one-sided. The first major U.S. victory occurred on the other side of the world. On May 1, an American fleet under Admiral George Dewey sailed into the harbor of Manila, in the Philippines, and sank the entire Spanish fleet in a matter of hours. Closer to home, about 17,000 U.S. troops stormed into Cuba. Some of them saw heavy action. On July 17, 1898, the city of Santiago, Cuba, surrendered, and the war was over. American forces occupied the Spanish colony of Puerto Rico shortly before an official armistice was signed on August 12.

The peace treaty between Spain and the United States was signed in Paris on December 10, 1898. This treaty made the United States a colonial power and dissolved the Spanish Empire. Cuba was freed from Spain but placed under the protection of the United States. Puerto Rico and the island of Guam, in the Pacific, were given to the United States as compensation for American losses in the war. The Philippines were surrendered to the United States for a payment of $20 million.

The United States emerged from this brief war as a world power with strong positions in Latin America and Asia. America continued to expand its territories elsewhere in the Pacific region by formally annexing Hawaii (which Cleveland had refused to do) as well as part of the Samoan Islands.

One of McKinley's most important achievements in the Caribbean was the Hay-Pauncefote Treaty with Great Britain, approved in 1901. By this treaty, Britain gave up all claims it had to any canal that might be built in the future across Panama; the United States would have exclusive ownership of any such canal. A few years later, America began building the Panama Canal.

★ ★

Open Door in China

The U.S. Senate ratified the Treaty of Paris (the treaty ending the Spanish-American War) in 1899, after which McKinley's secretary of state, John Hay, turned his attention to China. In 1899, Russia, Germany, France, and Great Britain were all scrambling to seize territory in China, which had been defeated in a war with Japan. Hay persuaded these powers to allow all nations to trade in China, creating in effect, an open-door policy. This agreement gave the United States a small foothold in Asia.

In 1900, a revolution broke out in China. Called the Boxer Rebellion, it threatened foreigners living in China. In response, McKinley sent a contingent of American troops to protect the foreign community.

McKinley's Second Term

By 1900, McKinley's foreign policy successes and the growing economic prosperity at home had made him a formidable candidate for re-election. He won renomination for president easily.

The real fireworks at the convention, however, came over the choice of vice-president. Vice-President Garret Hobart had died in office in 1899. Marcus Hanna reluctantly decided to give the nomination to New York's youthful governor, Theodore Roosevelt. In Hanna's view, Roosevelt, a hero of the Spanish-American War, was unreliable and even unstable. But Hanna thought that Roosevelt would cause far less trouble in what was then a powerless office—that of vice-president—than as governor of the most powerful state in the Union.

The McKinley-Roosevelt ticket swept to an easy victory in November, winning almost 900,000 more popular votes than the Democrats, who were headed once again by William Jennings Bryan. In the Electoral College, the Republicans won 292 votes to the Democrats' 155.

★ ★

McKinley was assassinated shortly after the start of his second term.

A prosperous and contented nation looked forward to the president's second term. In September 1901, McKinley journeyed to Buffalo, New York, to speak at the Pan-American Exposition. On September 6, he attended a public reception in the Temple of Music at the exposition. Hundreds of people lined up to shake his hand. One of the guests, Leon Czolgosz, approached McKinley wearing what seemed to be a bandage over his right hand. In fact, within the bandage was a gun. As the president extended his hand, Czolgosz fired, hitting him twice in the stomach.

Although gravely wounded, at first the president appeared likely to recover. But he took a turn for the worse, and on September 14, 1901, McKinley died at the age of 58, only six months into his second four-year term.

★ ★

Theodore Roosevelt
26th President of the United States

Term: *September 14, 1901–March 4, 1909; Republican*
First Lady: *Edith Kermit Carow Roosevelt*
Vice-President: *Charles W. Fairbanks*

5

★   ★   ★

Theodore Roosevelt

Theodore Roosevelt was only 42 years old when he became president. Not only was "Teddy"—as he was known to the American people—the youngest man ever to hold the office, but he was unlike any president the country had seen before. Sporting a full head of hair and his famous toothy grin, he gave off a sense of tremendous energy and enthusiasm. His young family filled the White House with noise and laughter. Within a short time, Roosevelt became one of the most beloved of American presidents.

Teddy Roosevelt continued the traditions and policies of William McKinley, but with a youthful, more vigorous style. He also expanded the powers of the presidency and made it, in his own words, a "bully pulpit"—a position used to persuade people and bring about change.

Roosevelt as a member of Harvard's track team

Early Life

Theodore Roosevelt was born in New York City on October 27, 1858. The Roosevelts were a distinguished family of Dutch descent who had emigrated to New Amsterdam in the 1640s. Theodore, who was called Teedie as a child, was the second of four children. Sickly from birth, he had very poor eyesight and suffered from asthma. At times, he found it difficult to breathe and would spend the night sitting up in bed.

When Teedie was 12, his father built a gymnasium for him in their home and urged the boy to build up his frail body. Young Roosevelt followed his father's advice, and by the time he was 15, he had developed a strong physique and had overcome his childhood asthma. Throughout his life, Roosevelt remained an advocate of strenuous exercise and enjoyed pushing himself to the limit.

In 1876, Roosevelt entered Harvard University. While in his senior year, he fell in love with Alice Hathaway Lee. In 1880, shortly after his graduation, they were married and settled in New York City.

Politics and Sorrow

Roosevelt developed an interest in politics and, at the age of 23, was elected to the New York state legislature on the Republican ticket. He soon achieved a reputation as a fearlessly honest politician and reformer.

In February 1884, tragedy struck. Alice Roosevelt died two days after giving birth to their first child, who was named Alice.

★ ★

On the very same day of his wife's death, Roosevelt's mother, Martha Bulloch Roosevelt, also died. The deaths of his wife and mother were a staggering blow.

At the end of 1884, Roosevelt decided not to run for re-election. Leaving his infant daughter in the care of his oldest sister, Anna, Roosevelt left New York and moved to his ranch in North Dakota. For the next two years, he raised cattle, hunted, and lived the life of a frontiersman. He also began writing a history book, which he called *The Winning of the West*.

Return to Public Office

Roosevelt returned from North Dakota in 1886 and journeyed to London, England, for a happy occasion: Putting his sorrows behind him, he married an old childhood friend, Edith Kermit Carow, on December 2. The newlyweds returned to the United States and settled at a home named Sagamore Hill, in Oyster Bay, Long Island, New York.

In 1889, the Republicans returned to the White House, and Roosevelt was offered a job on the Civil Service Commission by President Benjamin Harrison. He held this position for six years and was noted for his vigorous support of additional civil service reforms (reforms made to require that government jobs be given for skill, not as rewards for support).

Roosevelt returned to New York City in 1895 to become police commissioner. As the head of the city's police force, he fought against crime and corruption in politics. At times, he would disguise himself in a black cloak and a wide-brimmed hat and patrol the streets at night to discover firsthand what was going on. Many of his efforts, however, were opposed by politicians.

In 1897, Roosevelt returned to Washington after President McKinley appointed him assistant secretary of the navy. Naval affairs were a special interest of Roosevelt's. He predicted that the United States would eventually go to war with Spain, and on his own, he started to prepare the navy for war. Once the Spanish-American War broke out, Roosevelt resigned from his navy job and, with Leonard Wood, organized a regiment of volunteers to go and fight.

Rough Rider and Governor

These soldiers—the 1st Regiment of U.S. Cavalry Volunteers— came to be called the Rough Riders because most were ranchers and cowboys from the West. The actual command of the regiment went to Colonel Leonard Wood, a professional army man and a friend of Roosevelt's. Roosevelt received the rank of lieutenant colonel.

Transportation difficulties caused most of the regiment's horses to be stranded in Florida. As a result, the volunteers fought mostly on foot. Although they fought in the battle at Santiago, Cuba, they are legendary for their charge up Kettle Hill, which was later incorrectly called San Juan Hill. History, however, will forever remember Roosevelt as the hero of San Juan Hill.

Because of his exploits in Cuba during the summer of 1898, Roosevelt became an instant celebrity—and a candidate highly desired by New York's Republican party. Only a few months after his army service in the Spanish-American War ended, Roosevelt was nominated to run for governor of New York. In November, just a few days after his fortieth birthday, he was elected governor of New York.

New York's powerful Republican senator, Thomas C. Platt, had supported Roosevelt's candidacy. Once Roosevelt assumed office, however, Platt began to be alarmed. The young governor had all sorts of unconventional ideas about political reform, and he had a unique ability to draw publicity to himself. When Governor Roosevelt proposed a tax on corporations, Platt realized that he had a problem on his hands.

★ ★

Roosevelt and the Rough Riders became heroes for their fighting during the Spanish-American War.

In 1900, Platt saw an opportunity to move Roosevelt out of the governor's office and into a position where he could do no harm—the vice-presidency of the United States. President Mc-Kinley's chief campaign advisor, Marcus Hanna, also regarded Roosevelt as troublesome and dangerous. He agreed with Platt and had the Republican Convention nominate Roosevelt as McKinley's running mate in the 1900 election.

Rise to the White House

President McKinley was overwhelmingly re-elected to a second term and was sworn in on March 4, 1901. Beside him on the steps of the Capitol stood a somber-faced Theodore Roosevelt, who understood that he had been "kicked upstairs" by the party bosses. For the dynamic young leader, the vice-presidency held little attraction. The office had only one official responsibility—

★ ★

★ ★ ★ ★ ★ ★ ★ 🦅 ★ ★ ★ ★ ★ ★ ★

First Lady Edith Roosevelt

Edith Carow was born in Connecticut in 1861. Her parents, Charles and Gertrude Carow, were wealthy members of New York and Connecticut society. They spent most of the year at their brownstone home in New York City, just a few blocks from the Roosevelts' home. Young Edith was a playmate of Teddy Roosevelt's younger sister, Corinne.

Edith Kermit Carow Roosevelt

Edith attended Miss Comstock's School, a finishing school for wealthy young girls, and she often spent part of the summer with the Roosevelt children at Oyster Bay, Long Island. Edith was invited to Roosevelt's wedding to Alice Hathaway Lee in 1880. Their paths crossed again in 1885, a year after he had become a widower. He and Edith soon fell in love and were married in London, England, in December 1886.

Over the next ten years, the couple had four sons and a daughter—Theodore, Jr., Kermit, Ethel, Archibald, and Quentin—and Mrs. Roosevelt became a loving stepmother to Roosevelt's daughter Alice. Edith was with her husband when he heard the news of McKinley's death. The young mother now found herself and her family thrust into the limelight of the White House.

Mrs. Roosevelt did everything in her power to shield her family from publicity. The country was interested in the dynamic young family, but the First Lady wanted her children to grow up as normally as possible. Alice provided enough publicity for the whole family, however. In 1906, she married Nicholas Longworth, a Congressman, who was many years her senior, in a spectacular White House wedding.

Edith's sound judgment and even temper perfectly balanced her husband's boyish exuberance. In 1902, shortly after moving into the White House, she supervised a large-scale restoration of the mansion. She also established the First Ladies' portrait gallery on the first floor of the White House.

Mrs. Roosevelt traveled widely with her husband after he left office in 1909, but she always returned home to Sagamore Hill. In late 1918 and then in early 1919, she suffered a double tragedy: Quentin was shot down in a plane over France in the final days of World War I. Just a few weeks later, Teddy died in his sleep at Sagamore Hill.

The First Lady outlived her husband by almost 30 years. She spent her final years doing charity work in Oyster Bay and volunteering at nearby Christ Church. She died in 1948 at the age of 87 and is buried next to President Roosevelt at Sagamore Hill.

to preside over the Senate—and no power at all. Since McKinley was only 57 and in robust health, Roosevelt prepared himself for the four long years ahead.

All that changed six months later, however, when President McKinley was shot while on a visit to Buffalo. After struggling bravely for eight days, McKinley finally died. Like everything else in his life, Roosevelt's accession to the presidency was swift and filled with drama. The 42-year-old president soon let it be known that it was no longer business as usual in Washington.

Trustbuster and Reformer

Roosevelt called his program the Square Deal. One of his first moves was to attack a kind of monopoly called a trust (several companies joined together to eliminate competition). In 1902, he ordered the Justice Department to file suit against the North-ern Securities Company, which was a monopoly made up of three large railroads. The suit charged that they had committed "conspiracies in restraint of trade."

Other suits were later filed against big corporations, such as the United States Steel Corporation and the Standard Oil Company. Roosevelt wanted not to destroy these companies but to correct their worst excesses and to give other companies a fair opportu-nity to compete with them.

In his actions against the monopolies, Roosevelt followed the calls of a group of reformers and writers he named "muckrakers." He took the name from a character in John Bunyan's *Pilgrim's Progress* who could look no way but downward. With a muck-rake in his hand, he was interested only in raking the filth. The muckrakers of the early 1900s looked into business and brought injustices to the public eye.

The best-known muckrakers were Ida Tarbell, whose *History of the Standard Oil Company* exposed the unlawful practices of

★ ★

This political cartoon depicts Theodore Roosevelt cleaning up the muck in a meat-packing industry scandal.

this large organization, and Upton Sinclair, whose book *The Jungle* brought to light the terrible conditions in the meat-packing industry. With Roosevelt's support, Sinclair's work contributed to the passage of the Meat Inspection Act and the Pure Food and Drug Act of 1906.

Roosevelt also took a serious interest in the welfare of laborers. In 1902, coal miners belonging to the United Mine Workers went on strike in Pennsylvania. The mine owners refused to negotiate with the union. As the winter approached, Roosevelt threatened to call out the troops to operate the mines unless the owners agreed to arbitration (allowing a neutral third party to decide on a settlement). Using his bully pulpit, Roosevelt pressured the mine owners to accept the verdict of a commission appointed by him to settle the dispute.

Conservationist

The conservation of the nation's forests and wildlife became one of the major objectives of Roosevelt's administration. During the course of his presidency, he placed almost 125 million acres of government timberland under the protection of the National Forest Service, which was headed by the great conservationist Gifford Pinchot. Roosevelt's actions prevented the government from selling these lands to private developers, who would cut down the trees for lumber and paper.

In 1902, Congress passed at Roosevelt's request the National Reclamation Act (also known as the Newlands Act). This law encouraged the development of federal irrigation projects in dry areas of the country. In many respects, the modern environmental movement at the government level began with the presidency of Theodore Roosevelt.

Triumphant Re-election

By 1904, Roosevelt seemed sure to be re-elected. He was clearly someone who loved being president and who was adept at using the powers of the presidency to advance the causes he believed in.

The Republican Convention enthusiastically nominated Roosevelt for president. To fill the vacant office of vice-president, they chose Senator Charles W. Fairbanks of Indiana. The Democrats nominated Alton B. Parker, a New York judge, to face Roosevelt, but he never had a chance. Roosevelt swept back into office with a popular vote of 7.6 million to Parker's 5 million and 336 electoral votes to Parker's 140. At that time, it was the greatest victory in a presidential election there had ever been.

On the night of the election, an excited Roosevelt met the press and declared that he would honor the two-term tradition begun by President George Washington and not be a candidate for re-election in 1908. It was a promise he would later regret.

Vice-President Charles W. Fairbanks

Carrying the "Big Stick"

In foreign affairs, Roosevelt solidified U.S. gains in the Spanish-American War and increased American power and influence abroad. His policies were most controversial in the Caribbean region, where he often intervened on behalf of what he believed were America's best interests. His philosophy was to "speak softly and carry a big stick"—the "big stick" being a strong U.S. Army and Navy.

In 1902, three European powers—Great Britain, Germany, and Italy—began blockading and shelling Venezuelan ports because of loans that had not been repaid by the government of Venezuela. Fearing that these countries would seize territory in South America and violate the Monroe Doctrine, Roosevelt protested and pressured the countries to settle the dispute peacefully. Roosevelt's involvement made it clear that the United States would not tolerate European military power in the Western Hemisphere.

Other of Roosevelt's interventions were more controversial. The Hay-Pauncefote Treaty had opened the way for the building of a canal across Panama to connect the Atlantic Ocean and the Caribbean Sea with the Pacific Ocean. A treaty signed in 1903—

The events that led to the building of the Panama Canal resulted in controversy for the United States.

the Hay-Herrán Treaty—granted the United States the right to build the canal. At the time, Panama was a part of Colombia. The Colombian Senate, however, refused to approve the treaty.

At the same time, Panamanian rebels were trying to free Panama from Colombian control. Roosevelt ordered the U.S. Navy to keep any military forces away from Panama—in this case, the Colombian Army, which might advance to crush the revolt. A few days after the Panamanians revolted, the United States recognized the independence of Panama, and the new nation gave the United States control of a ten-mile-wide strip of land, which would be used to build the canal.

The South American nations were outraged at the United States for taking the side of the Panamanian rebels and meddling in Colombian affairs. In 1921, the United States paid $25 million to Colombia as compensation for its illegal military actions during the revolt in 1903. But Roosevelt had secured the land for the canal, and its construction began shortly thereafter.

Peacemaker

During his presidency, Roosevelt played a key role as an international peacemaker. In 1905, he arranged a conference in New Hampshire to end a war between Russia and Japan. For his efforts, he won the 1906 Nobel Peace Prize.

Roosevelt also helped settle a dispute between France and Germany over their interests in Morocco. The Algeciras Conference in 1906 averted war between these two European powers. Roosevelt was also active in planning the Second Hague Peace Conference in 1907, at which 46 nations agreed to rules concerning the peaceful settlement of international disputes. In 1908, Secretary of State Elihu Root concluded an agreement with Japan by which the United States and Japan agreed to respect each other's interests in the Pacific and to continue the open-door policy in China.

★ ★

Restless Retirement

Roosevelt had promised not to seek a third term in 1908. His power within the party was so great that he handpicked his successor, William Howard Taft, for the Republican presidential nomination. Taft was easily elected president in November 1908.

However, Roosevelt clearly would have loved to run for another term. He was only 50 years old and too young to retire, and he was filled with energy and ideas. When he left office on March 4, 1909, he decided to leave the country for a while in order to give Taft a chance to establish his own administration.

Roosevelt began a yearlong hunting trip through Africa. In March 1910, he met up with Mrs. Roosevelt in the Sudan. From there, the couple traveled throughout Europe, where they were greeted by royalty as well as by enthusiastic crowds eager to see the famous American president.

Later that year, Roosevelt returned to the United States—and was soon drawn back into politics. By this time, he had begun to feel that President Taft was too conservative and that he was not being true to Roosevelt's policies. After some thought, Roosevelt decided to challenge Taft for the Republican nomination for president in 1912.

Bull Moose Candidate

Taft and his supporters, however, controlled the Republican National Convention, and despite Roosevelt's popularity, Taft was renominated. A furious Roosevelt and his supporters stormed out of the convention and formed a new party—the National Progressive party. When reporters asked him how he felt, Roosevelt replied, "As fit as a bull moose." Thereafter, his party was known as the Bull Moose party.

Roosevelt knew that he had little chance of being elected, but he nonetheless decided to wage a strenuous campaign. He

★ ★

embarked on a tiring two-month speaking tour of the nation and bitterly attacked Taft Republicans wherever he went.

With the Republican party so divided, the Democrats won the election. In November 1912, Woodrow Wilson, the Democratic candidate, was elected president. Roosevelt came in second, but he managed to get only 88 electoral votes to Wilson's 435. Taft came in far behind, receiving only 8 electoral votes.

Disappointed by Taft's administration, Roosevelt returned to national politics as a Bull Moose candidate.

The Final Years

When World War I broke out in Europe in 1914, Roosevelt urged the Congress and the American people to prepare for war. Americans, however, did not want to get involved in European wars, and President Wilson did everything in his power to keep America out of the conflict.

The United States was finally drawn into the war in April 1917. Roosevelt had been assembling a division as early as 1916, and he offered his services to President Wilson. Wilson, however, hated Roosevelt and flatly refused to utilize him in any capacity. Bitterly disappointed and frustrated, Roosevelt sat out the war at Sagamore Hill.

His four sons, however, enlisted and saw combat. His youngest, Quentin, was an aviator. In July 1918, he was shot down in France. The loss of his beloved "Quenikins" was a blow from which Roosevelt never recovered. Six months later, on January 6, 1919, Roosevelt died in his sleep at Sagamore Hill.

★ ★

During the late 1890s and early 1900s, America emerged as a major industrial power.

6

★ ★ ★

The Beginning of the Modern Presidency

After a period of decline following the end of the Civil War in 1865, the presidency began to emerge as a powerful institution of government between 1889 and 1909. This change was due in part to the country's growth. As America was industrialized and became a major power, it faced crises at home and abroad that required strong executive leadership.

The Harrison Legacy

Benjamin Harrison was perhaps the most conservative and traditional of the presidents in the years from 1889 to 1909. Although he personally favored a less active role for the presidency, a number of important bills were passed during his term that were to have significant consequences for the future.

In 1890, Congress passed the McKinley Tariff Act and the Sherman Silver Purchase Act. Both measures had their supporters, but they were also violently opposed by some. Farmers, for example, resented the protection that the tariff bill gave to industry because they believed that it raised prices on the manufactured goods they had to buy. Still, the passage of these acts helped to start a debate that went on for the remainder of the 1890s. During Harrison's presidency, the United States grew dramatically, with six new states entering the Union between 1889 and 1890. Under him, the nation remained at peace abroad.

The Cleveland Legacy

Grover Cleveland had been president once before when he arrived at the White House in 1893. His second term was not as lucky as his first. Within a few months of his return to office, the nation was plunged into a financial crisis that led to an economic depression. For the remainder of Cleveland's term, the country's economy was in decline. Unemployment rose and hardship struck farmers across the nation.

Despite this, Cleveland remained popular with the people because of his unshakable honesty and commitment to principle. Nevertheless, he was unwilling to extend presidential power—both at home and abroad—even in an emergency. Cleveland alienated large sections of his party, dividing it to the point that it was defeated in the 1896 presidential election.

Cleveland's legacy is mixed. He was a man of principle but also a president who used his power too cautiously, if at all.

The McKinley Legacy

In many respects, William McKinley was the first modern president. He was a superb politician—shrewd, crafty, and willing to use his power when necessary. Although he was a traditional

U.S. Marines were sent to China to protect foreigners during the Boxer Rebellion.

Republican on such issues as the tariff and the gold standard, McKinley expanded the power of the presidency.

Most of McKinley's four and a half years in office were devoted to foreign affairs. McKinley led the nation into a war with Spain that resulted in the acquisition by the United States of a number of overseas territories. America also intervened in the Boxer Rebellion in China and worked toward keeping an open-door policy

★ ★

in that country, a policy that allowed U.S. business to gain a foot-hold in Asia.

McKinley was a popular president and the first one to be re-elected to a consecutive second term since Ulysses Grant's second election in 1872. But McKinley's second term was short-lived, as an assassin's bullet ended his life in 1901.

The Roosevelt Legacy

Theodore Roosevelt captured the imagination of the American people as no other president had ever done before. At 42, he was the youngest chief executive in the nation's history. Like McKinley, he was not afraid to use and extend the power of the presidency. But he differed from McKinley in a number of ways.

First, he was able to use publicity to enhance the power of the presidency. Roosevelt was young and enthusiastic. He won the hearts of the American people with his boundless energy, flash-ing grin, and outspoken support for many popular reforms.

Second, he was interested in domestic reform. He took on the trusts, passed legislation to protect America's natural resources, and pushed for laws that guarded the interests of labor. Roose-velt was actually a more politically conservative president than he appeared to be. Yet, because of his commitment to certain issues, he seemed always to be on the side of the common man, and the public loved him for it.

★ ★

GLOSSARY

bully pulpit A term used by President Theodore Roosevelt to describe the persuasive powers of the presidency.

Boxer Rebellion A revolution in China that resulted in President William McKinley's sending in U.S. troops to protect foreigners.

Electoral College The group that formally elects the president and vice-president by casting electoral votes. Members of the Electoral College are elected by popular vote—the vote of the people—in each state.

McKinley Tariff A tariff passed by Congress in 1890 that imposed high taxes on foreign imports.

muckrakers Writer-journalist reformers who exposed abuses in industries in the early 1900s.

National Reclamation Act An act passed by Congress to encourage irrigation projects.

Northern Securities case An antitrust case begun under President Roosevelt in 1902.

Panama Canal A human-made waterway across Panama built by the United States in the early 1900s.

Panic of 1893 A financial crisis in 1893 that led to a major economic depression.

Pullman strike A major labor action in 1894 that was crushed by federal troops.

Sherman Silver Purchase Act An act passed by Congress in 1890 that authorized the federal government to buy all the silver on the market.

Spanish-American War A conflict between the United States and Spain in 1898. Spain was defeated and the United States acquired an overseas empire in the Pacific and Caribbean regions.

Square Deal President Roosevelt's programs of reform.

tariff A tax imposed by a government on imports or exports.

CHRONOLOGY

1888	Benjamin Harrison is elected president.
1889–1890	Six new states are admitted to the Union.
1890	Congress passes the McKinley Tariff Act.
	Congress passes the Sherman Silver Purchase Act.
1892	Grover Cleveland is re-elected to a second term as president.
1893	The Panic of 1893 shakes U.S. finances and leads to economic depression.
	The Sherman Silver Purchase Act is repealed.
1894	Pullman Railroad strike occurs.
1896	William McKinley is elected president.
1898	The United States defeats Spain in the Spanish-American War and acquires many overseas territories.
	The Treaty of Paris between the United States and Spain ends the Spanish-American War.
1900	McKinley is re-elected president.
1901	McKinley is assassinated. Vice-President Theodore Roosevelt becomes president.
	The Hay-Pauncefote Treaty opens the way for the United States to build a canal across Panama.
1902	Roosevelt's Justice Department begins to file suit against large trusts and monopolies.
	Congress passes the National Reclamation Act, which encourages the development of irrigation projects.
1903	The Hay-Herrán Treaty grants the United States the right to build a canal across Panama.
1904	Roosevelt is re-elected to a full term of his own.
1905	Roosevelt sponsors a peace conference in New Hampshire to settle the war between Russia and Japan.
1906	Roosevelt wins the Nobel Peace Prize for helping settle the war between Russia and Japan.
1908	U.S.-Japanese agreement allows the open-door policy in China to continue.
1909	Roosevelt leaves office and is succeeded by William Howard Taft.

FURTHER READING

Clinton, Susan B. *Benjamin Harrison: 23rd President of the United States.* Chicago: Children's Press, 1989.

Kent, Zachary. *Grover Cleveland: 22nd and 24th President of the United States.* Chicago: Children's Press, 1989.

————. *William McKinley: 25th President of the United States.* Chicago: Children's Press, 1988.

Parks, E. W. *Teddy Roosevelt: All-Round Boy.* New York: Macmillan, 1989.

————. *Teddy Roosevelt: Young Rough Rider.* New York: Aladdin, 1989.

Pascoe, Elaine. *First Facts About the Presidents.* Woodbridge, CT: Blackbirch Press, 1996.

Roosevelt, Theodore. *The Autobiography of Theodore Roosevelt.* New York: Octagon, 1975.

Spies, Karen. *Our Presidency.* Brookfield, CT: Millbrook Press, 1994.

Steins, Richard. *Our National Capital.* Brookfield, CT: Millbrook Press, 1994.

Weber, Michael. *Our Congress.* Brookfield, CT: Millbrook Press, 1994.

Timeline

•1770•

1774 First Continental Congress

1775 American Revolution begins

1776 America declares independence from Great Britain

•1780•

1783 Treaty of Paris formally ends American Revolution

1787 U.S. Constitution is written

1789 George Washington becomes president

•1790•

1791 Bill of Rights becomes part of Constitution

1793 Eli Whitney invents cotton gin

1797 John Adams becomes president

•1800• Washington, D.C., becomes permanent U.S. capital

1801 Thomas Jefferson becomes president

1803 Louisiana Purchase almost doubles size of the United States

1808 Slave trade ends

1809 James Madison becomes president

•1810•

1812 War of 1812 begins

1814 British burn Washington, D.C. War of 1812 fighting ends

1815 Treaty of Ghent officially ends War of 1812

1817 James Monroe becomes president

•1820• Missouri Compromise is passed

1823 Monroe Doctrine is issued

1825 John Quincy Adams becomes president

1828 Popular votes used for first time to help elect a president

1829 Andrew Jackson becomes president

•1830• Indian Removal Act is passed by Congress

1832 Samuel Morse has idea for telegraph

1835 Samuel Colt patents revolver

1837 Martin Van Buren becomes president

1838 Native Americans are forced to move to Oklahoma traveling Trail of Tears

•1840•

1841 William Harrison becomes president
John Tyler becomes president

1845 James Polk becomes president
Texas is annexed to United States

1846 Mexican War begins
Boundary between Canada and United States is decided

1848 Gold is discovered in California
First women's rights convention is held

1849 Zachary Taylor becomes president

•1850• Millard Fillmore becomes president
Compromise of 1850 is passed

1853 Franklin Pierce becomes president

1857 James Buchanan becomes president

•1860• Southern states begin to secede from Union

1861 Abraham Lincoln becomes president

1863 Abraham Lincoln gives Gettysburg Address

1865 Andrew Johnson becomes president
Civil War ends
Freedmen's Bureau is created
13th Amendment abolishes slavery

1868 Impeachment charges are brought against President Johnson

1869 Ulysses S. Grant becomes president

•1870•

1873 U.S. economy collapses; depression begins

1876 Alexander Graham Bell invents telephone

1877 Rutherford Hayes becomes president

1879 Thomas Edison invents lightbulb

•1880•

1881 James Garfield becomes president
Chester Arthur becomes president

1882 Chinese Exclusion Act restricts number of Chinese immigrants allowed into United States

1885 Grover Cleveland becomes president

1889 Benjamin Harrison becomes president

•1890• U.S. troops kill more than 200 Sioux and Cheyenne at Wounded Knee

1893 Grover Cleveland becomes president
Charles and J. Frank Duryea construct first car in the United States

1897 William McKinley becomes president

1898 Spanish-American War occurs

•1900•

1901 Theodore Roosevelt becomes president

1903 Orville and Wilbur Wright fly their plane at Kitty Hawk, North Carolina

1908 Henry Ford produces Model T

1909 William Taft becomes president

•1910•

1913 Woodrow Wilson becomes president

1914 Panama Canal opens

1917 America enters World War I

1919 World War I ends

•1920• 19th Amendment gives women right to vote

1921 Warren Harding becomes president

1923 Calvin Coolidge becomes president

1927 Charles Lindbergh makes first nonstop flight across Atlantic

1929 Herbert Hoover becomes president
Stock market crashes; America enters economic depression

•1930•

1933 Franklin Roosevelt becomes president

1939 World War II begins

•1940•

1941 Pearl Harbor is bombed; America enters World War II

1945 Harry Truman becomes president
United States drops atomic bombs on Hiroshima and Nagasaki; World War II ends
United Nations is formed

•1950• Korean War begins

1953 Dwight Eisenhower becomes president
Korean War ends

1954 Supreme Court orders desegregation of schools

1957 Soviet Union launches *Sputnik I*

1958 United States launches *Explorer I*
NASA is created

•1960•

1961 John Kennedy becomes president

1962 Cuban Missile Crisis

1963 Lyndon Johnson becomes president
March on Washington

1964 Civil Rights Act of 1964 is passed

1965 First U.S. troops sent to Vietnam War

1968 Martin Luther King, Jr. is assassinated

1969 Richard Nixon becomes president
Neil Armstrong is first person to walk on moon

•1970• First Earth Day is celebrated

1973 OPEC places oil embargo; fuel shortages result

1974 Nixon is first president to resign
Gerald Ford becomes president

1975 War in Vietnam ends

1976 America celebrates its bicentennial

1977 James Carter becomes president

1978 Camp David Accords are signed by leaders of Israel and Egypt

1979 U.S. embassy in Iran is attacked and hostages are taken

1981 Ronald Reagan becomes president
American hostages are released
Reagan appoints first woman to Supreme Court, Sandra Day O'Connor

1986 U.S. space shuttle *Challenger* explodes after lift-off

1989 George Bush becomes president

•1990•

1991 Persian Gulf War occurs

1992 U.S. troops are sent to Somalia to lead multinational relief force
Riots explode in Los Angeles

1993 William Clinton becomes president
World Trade Center is bornbed by terrorists

1995 Bomb destroys federal building in Oklahoma City

•2000•

59

PRESIDENTS OF THE UNITED STATES

President	Birth	Party	Term	Death
George Washington	February 22, 1732; Westmoreland Cty., VA	None	April 30, 1789- March 4, 1797	December 14, 1799; Mt. Vernon, VA
John Adams	October 30, 1735; Braintree (Quincy), MA	Federalist	March 4, 1797- March 4, 1801	July 4, 1826; Quincy, MA
Thomas Jefferson	April 13, 1743; Albemarle Cty., VA	Democratic- Republican	March 4, 1801- March 4, 1809	July 4, 1826; Charlottesville, VA
James Madison	March 16, 1751; Port Conway, VA	Democratic- Republican	March 4, 1809- March 4, 1817	June 28, 1836; Orange County, VA
James Monroe	April 28, 1758; Westmoreland Cty., VA	Democratic- Republican	March 4, 1817- March 4, 1825	July 4, 1831; New York, NY
John Quincy Adams	July 11, 1767; Braintree (Quincy), MA	Democratic- Republican	March 4, 1825- March 4, 1829	February 23, 1848; Washington, D.C.
Andrew Jackson	March 15, 1767; Waxhaw, SC	Democratic	March 4, 1829- March 4, 1837	June 8, 1845; Nashville, TN
Martin Van Buren	December 5, 1782; Kinderhook, NY	Democratic	March 4, 1837- March 4, 1841	July 24, 1862; Kinderhook, NY
William Harrison	February 9, 1773; Berkeley, VA	Whig	March 4, 1841- April 4, 1841	April 4, 1841; Washington, D.C.
John Tyler	March 29, 1790; Charles City Cty., VA	Whig	April 4, 1841- March 4, 1845	January 18, 1862; Richmond, VA
James Polk	November 2, 1795; Mecklenburg Cty., NC	Democratic	March 4, 1845- March 4, 1849	June 15, 1849; Nashville, TN
Zachary Taylor	November 24, 1784; Orange Cty., VA	Whig	March 4, 1849- July 9, 1850	July 9, 1850; Washington, D.C.
Millard Fillmore	January 7, 1800; Locke Township, NY	Whig	July 9, 1850- March 4, 1853	March 8, 1874; Buffalo, NY
Franklin Pierce	November 23, 1804; Hillsborough, NH	Democratic	March 4, 1853- March 4, 1857	October 8, 1869; Concord, NH
James Buchanan	April 23, 1791; Cove Gap, PA	Democratic	March 4, 1857- March 4, 1861	June 1, 1868; Lancaster, PA
Abraham Lincoln	February 12, 1809; Hardin Cty., KY	Republican	March 4, 1861- April 15, 1865	April 15, 1865; Washington, D.C.
Andrew Johnson	December 29, 1808; Raleigh, NC	Republican	April 15, 1865- March 4, 1869	July 31, 1875; Carter County, TN
Ulysses Grant	April 27, 1822; Point Pleasant, OH	Republican	March 4, 1869- March 4, 1877	July 23, 1885; Mount McGregor, NY
Rutherford Hayes	October 4, 1822; Delaware, OH	Republican	March 4, 1877- March 4, 1881	January 17, 1893; Fremont, OH
James Garfield	November 19, 1831; Orange, OH	Republican	March 4, 1881- September 19, 1881	September 19, 1881; Elberon, NJ
Chester Arthur	October 5, 1830; North Fairfield, VT	Republican	September 20, 1881- March 4, 1885	November 18, 1886; New York, NY

President	Birth	Party	Term	Death
Grover Cleveland	March 18, 1837; Caldwell, NJ	Democratic	March 4, 1885-March 4, 1889; March 4, 1893-March 4, 1897	June 24, 1908; Princeton, NJ
Benjamin Harrison	August 20, 1833; North Bend, OH	Republican	March 4, 1889-March 4, 1893	March 13, 1901; Indianapolis, IN
William McKinley	January 29, 1843; Niles, OH	Republican	March 4, 1897-September 14, 1901	September 14, 1901; Buffalo, NY
Theodore Roosevelt	October 27, 1858; New York, NY	Republican	September 14, 1901-March 4, 1909	January 6, 1919; Oyster Bay, NY
William Taft	September 15, 1857; Cincinnati, OH	Republican	March 4, 1909-March 4, 1913	March 8, 1930; Washington, D.C.
Woodrow Wilson	December 28, 1856; Staunton, VA	Democratic	March 4, 1913-March 4, 1921	February 3, 1924; Washington, D.C.
Warren Harding	November 2, 1865; Corsica, OH	Republican	March 4, 1921-August 2, 1923	August 2, 1923; San Francisco, CA
Calvin Coolidge	July 4, 1872; Plymouth, VT	Republican	August 3, 1923-March 4, 1929	January 5, 1933; Northampton, MA
Herbert Hoover	August 10, 1874; West Branch, IA	Republican	March 4, 1929-March 4, 1933	October 20, 1964; New York, NY
Franklin Roosevelt	January 30, 1882; Hyde Park, NY	Democratic	March 4, 1933-April 12, 1945	April 12, 1945; Warm Springs, GA
Harry Truman	May 8, 1884; Lamar, MO	Democratic	April 12, 1945-January 20, 1953	December 26, 1972; Kansas City, MO
Dwight Eisenhower	October 14, 1890; Denison, TX	Republican	January 20, 1953-January 20, 1961	March 28, 1969; Washington, D.C.
John Kennedy	May 29, 1917; Brookline, MA	Democratic	January 20, 1961-November 22, 1963	November 22, 1963; Dallas, TX
Lyndon Johnson	August 27, 1908; Stonewall, TX	Democratic	November 22, 1963-January 20, 1969	January 22, 1973; San Antonio, TX
Richard Nixon	January 9, 1913; Yorba Linda, CA	Republican	January 20, 1969-August 9, 1974	April 22, 1994; New York, NY
Gerald Ford	July 14, 1913; Omaha, NE	Republican	August 9, 1974-January 20, 1977	
James Carter	October 1, 1924; Plains, GA	Democratic	January 20, 1977-January 20, 1981	
Ronald Reagan	February 6, 1911; Tampico, IL	Republican	January 20, 1981-January 20, 1989	
George Bush	June 12, 1924; Milton, MA	Republican	January 20, 1989-January 20, 1993	
William Clinton	August 19, 1946; Hope, AR	Democratic	January 20, 1993-	

INDEX

Boldfaced, italicized page numbers include picture references.

Roosevelt, Theodore
  birth of, 38
  and Bull Moose party, 48–*49*
  children of, 42, 49
  and Congress, 9
  death of, 42, 49
  early career of, 38–41
  early life of, *38*
  and elections, 41, 45, 48–*49*
  First Lady. (*see* Edith Roosevelt)
  and foreign affairs, 9, 46–47
  as governor of New York, 40–41
  legacy of, 54
  marriages of, 38, 39, 42
  Nobel Peace Prize for, 47
  as peacemaker, 47
  and presidency in twentieth
    century, 9
  as president, 43–*44*, 45, 46–47,
    55
  and Progressivism, *9*
  as reformer, 39, 40
  reputation of, 36, 54
  retirement of, 42, 48, 49
  and Rough Riders, 40, *41*
  and Taft, 48–49
  terms of, *36*
  as vice-president, 26, 34, 40,
    41, 43
  vice-president for. (*see* Charles
    W. Fairbanks)
  and Wilson, 49

Root, Elihu, 47
Rough Riders, 40, *41*
Russia, 34, 47

S

Samoan Islands, 33
San Juan Hill (Cuba), 40
Secret ballot, 7
Senate, U.S., 24, 34, 43
Senators, direct election of, 7
Settlement houses, *6*, *8*
Sherman Silver Purchase Act
  (1890), 15, *16*, 22, 52, 55
Silver, free, 15, *16*, 22, 25, 30,
  52, 55
Sinclair, Upton, 44
South Dakota, 16
Spain, 24–25. *See also* Spanish-
  American War
Spanish-American War, 27, *32*–33,
  34, 40, *41*, 46, 53, 55
Square Deal, 43, 55
Standard Oil Company, 43–44
State government, 7
Stevenson, Adlai E., 18, *20*
Strikes, 22–*23*, 44, 55

T

Taft, William Howard, 48–49

Tarbell, Ida, 43–44
Tariffs, 15, 29, 52, 53, 55
Taxes, 7, 39
Treaty of Paris (1898), 33
Trusts, 9, 43, 54, 55

U

United Mine Workers, 44
United States
  expansion of, 16, 52
  as major industrial power, *50*, 51
  as world power, 27, 33
United States Steel Corporation, 43

V

Venezuela, 25, 46

W

Wake Island, 33
Washington, George, 45
Washington (state), 16
Weaver, James, 20
White House, 14, 42
Wilson, Woodrow, 49
Wisconsin, 7
Wood, Leonard, 40
World War I, 49
Wyoming, 16